TopReaders

Dogs

Denise Ryan

Contents

There are hundreds of different breeds of dogs. They range from the tiny chihuahua to the Irish wolfhound, which is the tallest dog in the world.

Boxers

Boxers are bright and loyal .
They are good watchdogs.
Boxers need a lot of exercise.

This boxer is chewing on a bone.

Boxers are medium-size dogs
with smooth coats and
square-jawed muzzles .

boxer

muzzle

smooth coat

white markings

Great Danes

Great Danes are very large dogs. They are usually gentle and well behaved.

Great Danes were once used as hunting dogs.

Great Danes come in different colors and patterns.

Mastiffs

The first mastiffs were used for fighting and hunting. They are strong dogs and need firm training.

Mastiffs need a lot of exercise.

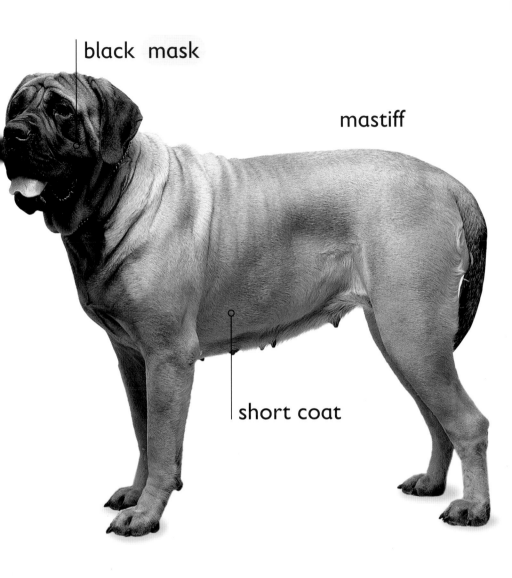

black mask

mastiff

short coat

Mastiffs are good guard dogs.
They are brave and loyal.

Search Dogs

Search dogs are specially trained to help find people who are lost or trapped after earthquakes or explosions.

search dog

Search dogs also help find lost children, walkers, and climbers.

Saint Bernards

Saint Bernards are famous rescue dogs. For hundreds of years, they have helped to find lost travelers in the snowy mountains of Switzerland .

Saint Bernards have white faces with dark brown and black markings.

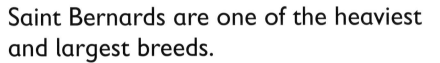

Saint Bernards are one of the heaviest and largest breeds.

Labradors

Labradors are good at finding things. They were bred to go into the water to collect ducks and to help bring in fishermen's nets.

black Labrador

Labradors have soft mouths and carry things very gently.

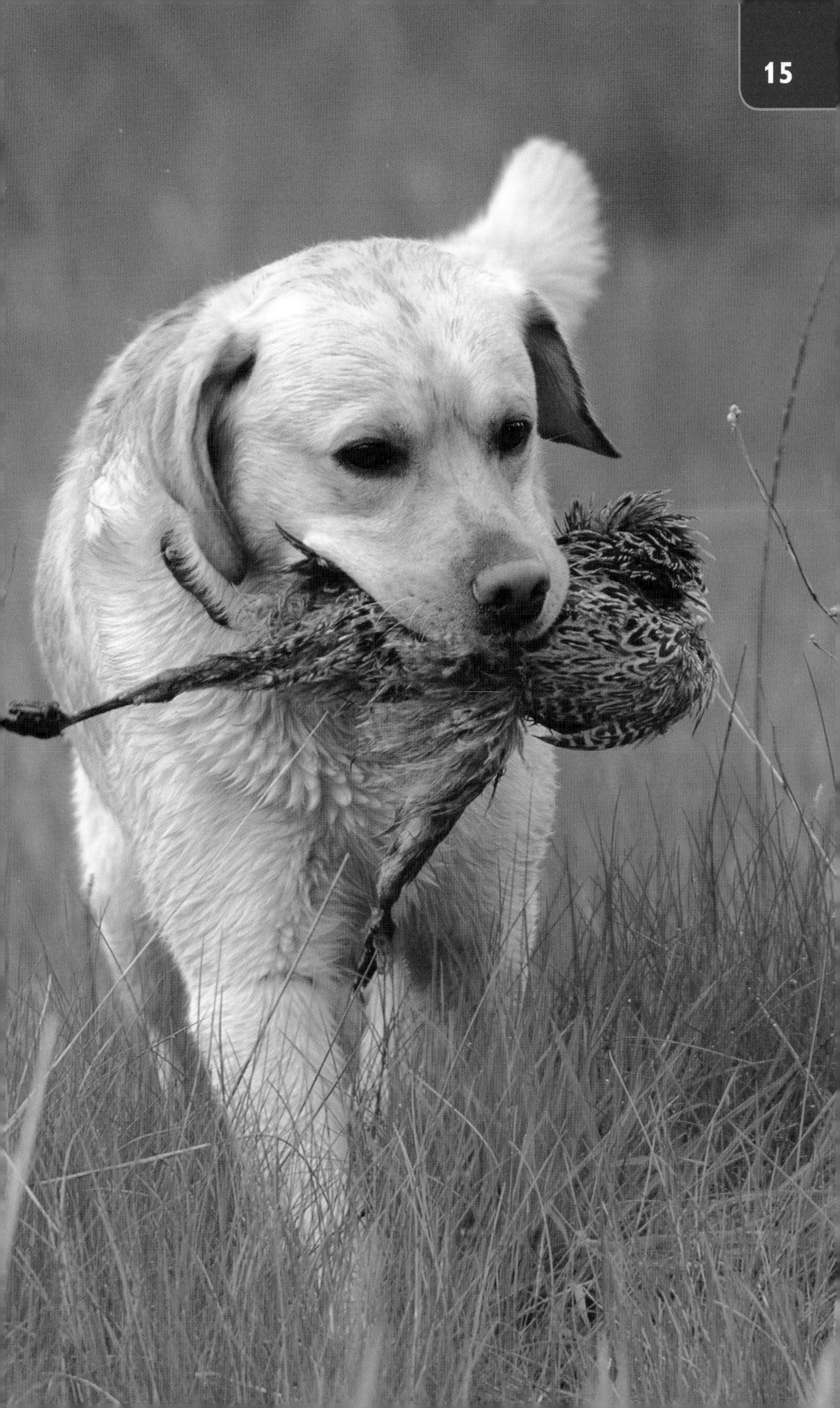

Sheep Dogs

Sheep dogs are working dogs.
They keep flocks of sheep together.

Two sheep dogs guard a flock of sheep.

This sheep dog
is a border collie.

Cattle Dogs

Cattle dogs are working dogs, too.
Their main job is to keep cattle
moving in the right direction.

a cattle dog at work

This Australian cattle dog
is called a blue heeler. They are
always alert and ready to work.

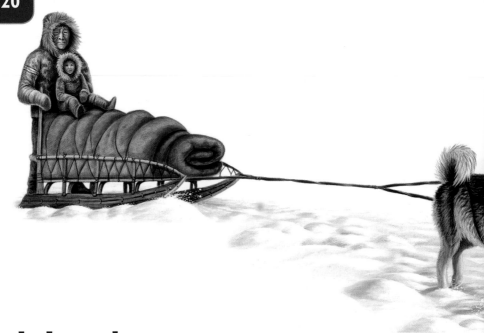

Huskies

Huskies are strong dogs with thick coats. They have white faces and ears shaped like triangles.

Huskies can pull loads across the snow. They often work in teams.

Huskies work in Alaska as sled dogs.

a team of huskies

Samoyeds

Samoyeds are friendly and gentle.
They were once used to pull sleds.
Today, they are used as pets.

The Samoyed
comes from
the Arctic .

Samoyeds have two coats.
Their undercoat is soft, thick wool.
Their outer coat has long, rough hair.

Pekingese

Pekingese have long, straight coats and flat, wrinkled faces.

flat face

The emperors of ancient China sometimes carried them in the sleeves of their robes.

long, straight coat

Poodles

Poodles are smart and loyal dogs.
They have thick, woolly coats.
Poodles come in different sizes
and colors.

This brown poodle
looks like a fluffy toy.

The hair of this poodle has been cut in a "lion clip."

Poodles were once used in circuses because they are easy to train.

Dalmatians

Dalmatians once ran next to horse-drawn carriages. They protected the passengers. They also kept the stables free of rats.

Dalmatians can have black or brown spots.

In America, Dalmatians sometimes live in firehouses. Many firefighters keep them as pets.

Quiz

Can you match the picture with the dog's name?

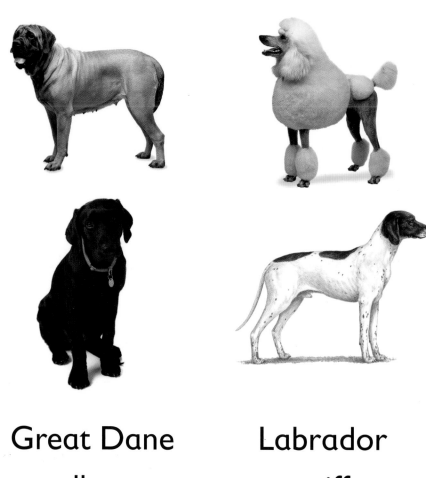

Great Dane

poodle

Labrador

mastiff

Glossary

Arctic: the area around the North Pole

breeds: groups of animals with a common background

emperors: the rulers of countries

firehouses: buildings for fire engines

flocks: groups of animals

guard: to keep something safe

loyal: faithful to an owner

mask: another word for a dog's face

muzzles: the snouts of some animals

outer: on the outside

sled: a vehicle on runners used over snow

Switzerland: a small mountainous country in Europe

undercoat: the coat that grows under another one

Index